Susan Katz Advantage
Create Your Dream Job: Change Your Mindset, Change Your Future

Susan B. Katz

The Omnibus Publishing
Baltimore, Maryland

Copyright © 2016 by Susan B. Katz.

All rights reserved. No part of this publication may be reproduced, distributed or transmitted in any form or by any means, including photocopying, recording, or other electronic or mechanical methods, without the prior written permission of the publisher, except in the case of brief quotations embodied in critical reviews and certain other non-commercial uses permitted by copyright law. For permission requests, inquire directly to the publisher, addressed "Attention: Permissions Coordinator," at the address below.

The Omnibus Publishing
5422 Ebenezer Rd.
PO Box 152
Baltimore, MD 21162
www.theomnibuspublishing.com.

Book Layout ©2015 BookDesignTemplates.com

Ordering Information:
Quantity sales. Special discounts are available on quantity purchases by corporations, associations, and others. For details, contact the "Special Sales Department" at the address above or email info@omnibuspub.com with "Special Sales Department" in the subject line.

Susan Katz Advantage. Create Your Dream Job: Change Your Mindset, Change Your Future/ Susan B. Katz. -- 1st ed.
ISBN 978-0-9966753-5-2

Contents

Preface VII

Introduction: The 10 Most Common Job Search Mistakes 3

Chapter 1   My Story 11

Part I   Understanding Your Beliefs and How They Affect Your Job Search

    Chapter 2   Alignment and Core Values: How You Are Wired and Why It Matters 19

    Chapter 3   Clarity: Figuring Out What You Really Want to Do 25

    Chapter 4   Mindset, Belief, and Behavior: What They Are and Why They Matter 37

    Chapter 5   Your Story: Understanding How Your Past Has Been Shaping Your Future 45

    Part II   Creating an Action Plan for Your Job Search

    Chapter 6   Building A Social Network that Works for You: Finding and Meeting the People in Your Network 59

Chapter 7 Learning to Ask Great Questions:
          Making the Most of Your Meetings with
          Networking Contacts..69

Chapter 8 Creating Your Plan and Sticking to It:
          The Right Level of Activity for You....................77

Chapter 9 Wrapping It Up: Reviewing Lessons Learned
          and Putting Your Plan into Action.....................81
Appendix..85

Dedication

This book is dedicated to all the people who are seeking meaningful work and a fulfilling career.

ACKNOWLEDGEMENTS

Writing a book is a long process requiring self-discipline and a great team who have complementary skills and who encourage, support and help throughout the process.

Thanks to the following individuals who without their encouragement, contributions and support this book would not have been written:

Henry Mortimer, Mortimer Communications, my writing coach who kept me on task and continually offered encouragement, feedback and editing.

Nancy Evans, Evans Editorial Services, a good friend who always sees the big picture and has the ability to help me see things more clearly.

Dana Knighten, Blue Herron, a very creative editor who added important structure to the book and did a great job making everything read better!

Wendy Dean, The Omnibus Publishing, who immediately solved the problem of "now that I wrote it, how do I get it published?" I'm thankful to have met Wendy.

Greg Scheingold, my business coach, who encouraged me to build a business when I left my corporate career and helped me become a much better coach.

Stephanie Limmer, Limmer Creative, who is always there to give me feedback, clarity and was instrumental in helping me finalize the title of the book.

Jim Allen, my husband, my best friend and my business partner who frequently gave me feedback and encouraged me to get this book done! Jim continually works with me and helps make every thing we do together better. Our business would not be where it is without our collaboration.

PREFACE

Who This Book Is For

Are you looking for a new job? Perhaps you've been part of a corporate layoff, your company decided you were no longer a fit for the job, or you decided you no longer like your job. Or perhaps you feel as if you are, or should be, a corporate refugee—either you're ready to flee the corporate world, or you're tired of working for a company where decisions are driven more by short-term shareholder value than by a long-term vision of what's right for the company. If any of these descriptions fits you, read on.

It's common for employees to dislike the work they are doing, disagree with company decisions, or dislike their boss or peers. Many people end up in such situations and feel overwhelmed about the prospect of finding a new job—one in which they are engaged, fulfilled, and respected in their work, AND in which they are realizing their full potential.

Although most people want to feel that they are making a meaningful contribution through their work, a recent Gallup poll found that only 30% of U.S. workers consider themselves fully engaged in their work. This translates directly into lost money for organizations and dissatisfaction for the majority of workers.

Some businesses understand that one of their most important assets is their people, and they do a great job of putting the company's long-term health at the forefront of decision-making.

However, today this seems to be more the exception than the rule. Unfortunately, many companies lack leadership, take a short-term view, and don't understand how properly aligning employees with their work, challenging them to grow, and helping them develop professionally are critical to the organization's long-term success.

As an employee, you have little or no control over how a company's leadership behaves—but you DO have control over the decisions you make regarding the company you work for and the job you choose.

What You'll Find In These Chapters

I wrote this book because I wanted to share with you some of the things I've learned and observed through my own experiences that can help you be more effective in your own job search.

Simply put, my goal is to help you do two things:
- Identify and avoid the behaviors that are likely to decrease the effectiveness of your job search.
- Increase the behaviors that will help your job search end in success.

In **Chapter 1**, I share part of my own story to demonstrate how the process you're about to learn worked for me, and the success I experienced as a result. **Part I** of this book (Chapters 2–5) focuses on helping you understand *why* what you think about has such a significant impact on your job search. **Part II** (Chapters 6–9) is tactical. Those chapters lead you step by step through the process of growing your social network, learning how to have productive conversations by asking great questions, and formulating a specific job search action plan. The **Appendix** at the end of this book contains a set of numbered worksheets to help you work through some of the chapter content. Chapters that have accompanying worksheets contain a box at the end of the chapter that lists those worksheets by name and number.

In **Parts I and II**, you'll find information about a process that will help you:

- gain clarity,
- change your behavior,
- create a realistic, positive mindset,
- grow and make effective use of your natural network, and
- develop a plan of action.

What you *won't* find is instructions on how to write the perfect resumé or cover letter, information about career counseling or job boards, or advice on how to send resumés blindly to potential employers. Numerous resources are available already to help you in those areas.

How to Get the Most Out of This Process

I strongly recommend that you read this book from beginning to end, even if some of the information at first seems unrelated to your situation. That way, you'll get a big-picture sense of the process and gain a better understanding of how each step and all the related exercises and worksheets are essential to helping you find your dream job.

Finding that job is going to require you to reach outside your comfort zone—but that's also when growth and fulfillment occur. Keep that in mind as you work through the strategies in this book. They may sometimes feel uncomfortable, but if you do them consistently and persistently, they will help you reach your goal.

Consistency and persistence are two behaviors that are critical to this process. Elite athletes and world-renowned musicians alike practice many hours each day for years on end before they become successful—and none of them allows poor performance on one day to derail them from ongoing practice, evaluation, and feedback to improve their future performance. They become elite only by putting in the effort, continually working to perfect their skills, and making mistakes along the way. None of these behaviors happens without the right mindset.

Whether you are looking for a new job, training to become an elite athlete, saving for the future, getting healthy, or building a business, thought creates your reality. Because mindset, your beliefs, and your thoughts are the foundation for anything you create in your life, the entirety of **Part I** is dedicated to them. Pay close attention to these chapters, and be sure to work through all the exercises.

I recommend that you create a written or electronic journal to record all of your responses. There's power in getting information out of your head and into a written format. If your thoughts stay only in your head, nothing is likely to change, because you'll get stuck in what I call "spin" or "swirl"—when your thoughts simply go around and around and take you nowhere. This book is meant not to become another "shelf help book" gathering dust on the shelf after you read it, but to be an action plan that helps you change your life.

Above all, I want to help you land your dream job as quickly and efficiently as possible—a job that offers the right fit for you and for the company you work for. Get started now by answering these questions:

- What work or personal activities are inside your comfort zone?
- What would you like to achieve professionally or personally that is outside your comfort zone?

INTRODUCTION

The 10 Most Common Job Search Mistakes

Job searching today is an understandably scary prospect. With all the news about the number of people who either are out of work, have stopped looking for work, or have resorted to part-time work, and the caution companies are showing in adding new positions, it would be easy to assume that sticking with an unfulfilling job is better than risking a search for a new one.

Making that assumption would be your first mistake!

Contrary to the bleak picture the news presents, there ARE jobs that need to be filled with people just like you. I see it all the time with my clients who need to hire new employees as their businesses grow. Those employers are motivated to find the right people for the jobs.

In my coaching business, I work primarily with business owners and executives. Along the way, though, I've also attracted a significant number of workers who want my help in figuring out what to do next, either because they hate their current job or they are out of work. Some of these people have included:

- A Teach for America teacher who did not want to stay in the program
- An attorney who was unhappy at her firm
- An accountant who wanted to move to a different partnership
- A digital marketing expert who had landed in an unsuccessful start-up (who later went on to start a new business!)
- A researcher who had divorced and relocated to be close to family and who was having a challenging time finding a new position

With each of the individuals mentioned above, I was able to help them gain clarity, discover how they are wired and what that meant in terms of aligning with their work, build their confidence, believe in possibilities rather than obstacles, develop a plan of action for systematically approaching their job search, and ultimately land their next job.

In the process of working with so many people, I began to recognize some common patterns that were emerging in terms of where people got stuck, what they found the most challenging, and which mistakes kept them from finding the fulfilling work they sought. I've distilled these patterns down to what I call "The 10 Most Common Job Search Mistakes." Learning about them now, before you begin this process, is the first step in changing your limiting beliefs to create the positive mindset you need to pursue your goals.

Mistake #1: Sending out resumes only in response to job postings.

This in itself is not a bad thing to do, but it's not likely to yield the quick results that tapping into your own personal and social network will produce. When you send out your resume blindly, you often end up competing with hundreds if not thousands of potential candidates. This makes it more difficult for you and your resumé to rise to the top of the pile. If you're already sending out resumes this way, then keep doing it—but don't rely on it as your only means of finding a job.

Are you aware that up to 60% of all open positions are filled through referrals (*HR News Daily, Dec 2012*)? If you only respond blindly to job postings, you're missing a huge opportunity. We all enjoy doing business with people we know, like, and trust—and we tend to trust people MUCH more quickly if another person we know and trust has referred them to us.

If you were an employer, would you be more likely to hire a referral from a trusted source, or someone who applied for the job through a job board? If you're like most people, you said the person who came to you through a trusted source.

Mistake #2: Not believing that it's possible to get a new job.

Over and over, I hear people say some version of this statement: "There's no way I can find a new job." Why do people hold onto such a counterproductive belief? There are many excuses and reasons:

> *The economy is bad... I don't have the right skills for the jobs that are out there... I don't have time to look while I'm working... I'm worried that my employer will find out I'm looking... I'm too old... I've sent out resumes and I never hear back from anyone, so why bother?*

If this sounds like you, it's time to examine your belief system to see what might be keeping you from a more positive outlook on your job search. Thoughts lead to emotions, and emotions in turn dictate behavior. If you keep having negative thoughts, I promise you that you will keep getting negative results.

Mistake #3: Not clearly defining the work that you want to do and are best suited to do.

The most common statement I hear from people is that they can't figure out what they want to do. Sometimes it's hard to figure out what job will be the right fit for you. I remember thinking this myself before I decided to start my own business. I'd been working in educational publishing, and although I knew I no longer wanted to stay in that field (a realization I'd come to 2 years before I was downsized), I didn't know what I wanted to do instead. What I really wanted was for someone else to give me the answer. I kept thinking to myself, "If only someone else would just make it easy and tell me the next thing to do!" Unfortunately, no one else can tell you what you consider your strengths, your passions, and your purpose. And although it takes some work to figure those things out, it can be done.

Job searching is a process that can take time, especially when you are searching for the RIGHT job—one that's a great fit for you and for the company, that is in full alignment with who you are, and that matches your interests.

Mistake #4: Being afraid to ask for referrals.

This happens to people searching for new jobs as well as to business owners or sales people looking to grow their business. We may be afraid to ask for help, have an underlying fear of being perceived as pushy, or believe most people are not interested in helping us. And to all of these, my response is, "So what!" Are you more concerned about how someone might perceive you, or about building your network to find a new job? If you are fearful of being too pushy, there are ways to ask for referrals that are not pushy. One of the best ways to start is to ask people for a 15 to 20 minute conversation to get their advice. Then, in the context of the conversation, you can ask who are the one or two people they know who would be good to speak with to help you further your job search.

Mistake #5: Avoiding conversations with people because you are embarrassed to be out of work.

I've spoken with people who have been out of work for a while, and rather than going to networking functions and talking with people, they hide at home behind their computers, sending out resumes and getting discouraged when nothing happens. I remember feeling embarrassed the first time I lost a job and needed to find another one. I had defined my self-worth by the work I had been doing. However, I quickly realized that I needed to swallow my pride, stop defining myself by my work, and start talking to people who might be able to help me find my next position. Action sets you free, and things happen when you engage with other people.

Mistake #6: Spending too much time on the wrong activities.

People who are looking for jobs often spend time on activities that are not likely to lead to finding a new job quickly, such as perfecting their cover letters or resumes and responding to job postings. Again, there's nothing intrinsically wrong with either of these activities, except when they are done to the exclusion of doing the right activities—networking and meeting with people who might be able to help you find a job.

Mistake #7: Talking too much when you have a networking one-to-one conversation or are meeting with a prospective employer.

This is a common problem with job seekers, sales people, start-up business owners, existing business owners, and many others. It's what I call "showing up and throwing up," and it often occurs because the person is nervous and believes he or she needs to be interesting. The key is to be *interested*—not *interesting*. You do that by asking questions and learning as much as you can about the other person. Being genuinely inquisitive and curious gives you the opportunity to build a stronger relationship with the person, and he or she will be more likely want to help you. As Stephen Covey said, "Seek to understand before being understood."

Mistake #8: Having difficulty asking questions or knowing what questions to ask.

Often we're afraid to ask questions because we think we're being intrusive or might ask the wrong questions. Or, we're afraid of the answers we might receive. It's critical that you learn to ask questions. As long as your questions are asked genuinely—meaning that you truly are interested in what the other person has to say—and are appropriate to the context of what the other person has already shared with you, you will not be perceived as intrusive or pushy. It's important to start out with some general questions that can be used in any situation. Then, by listening actively, you will be able to ask what I call "peel the onion" questions to help you gain a greater understanding of and more insight about the other person.

Mistake #9: Not using every conversation as an opportunity to expand your network.

The one cardinal rule when expanding your network is to ask, after each conversation, for introductions to one, two, or three people who might be good candidates to help you further your job search. Once again, most people worry that asking that type of question will seem pushy. If you approach the other person by asking for advice, most often they will be delighted to help you.

Mistake #10: Lacking confidence or feeling hopeless.

If you don't have confidence or belief in yourself, why should anyone else believe in you? This is critically important to your success in finding a new job. Remember, thoughts drive emotions, and emotions drive behavior. Whether you feel hopeless or hopeful, your behavior will reflect that feeling.

Keep in mind that even if you are unappreciated or not a fit at your current company, this is completely unrelated to how you will be perceived and perform at another company that has an entirely different set of values and a different culture. In a job that's truly aligned with who you are, you'll be able to thrive and make significant contributions to that company.

The chapters that follow will expand on these ideas in much more detail. As you work through the material, you'll have an opportunity to answer questions and explore exercises designed to help you apply the ideas to your own situation. Your honest answers will help you change your limiting behaviors and find the job that's right for you.

Remember, there's no right or wrong when it comes to your job search—only effective behavior and ineffective behavior. If your behavior is helping to lead you in the direction of finding a job, keep doing it. If your behavior is *not* helping to accomplish this, then it's causing you to be ineffective and it's time to find a new way of searching.

In the end, your behaviors and actions are measured by the result—finding a great job—not by how you go about it.

Good luck!

CHAPTER 1

My Story

In the late 1990s, after 20 successful years in a career I loved, I was forced to leave my job and look for a new one. I'd been an executive with a higher education publishing company, and for a variety of reasons, including some internal political struggles, my boss decided to move me out of my current job. He was kind enough to offer me a "fake" position in the company, one he created to keep me employed while I looked for work. I was given about six months to find a new job while I hung onto the "fake" one.

There I was: a divorced mom and primary breadwinner with two kids to support, facing the unknown.

Needless to say, I was panicked and scared. My biggest fear was that I wouldn't be able to provide for my family. I also wondered if I'd be able to find a job with pay equal to what I'd been earning—I knew executive-level jobs were scarce, and I wasn't sure if I'd be able to find another one. I also wasn't sure whether I wanted to stay in the publishing industry.

What I couldn't know then was that being forced to make the move would turn out so well. Not only would I land in a job where my knowledge was appreciated and move to a city I liked better than the one where I had been living, but also these very experiences ultimately would lead me to my current business—my passion and my calling.

What happened in the interim, between the shock of that lost job and where I am today, is the story of this chapter.

Finding My Dream Job

When I lost that publishing job, it felt like a death. I spent plenty of time grieving the loss of a position I loved and a set of relationships I'd developed during the years I worked for the company. At the same time, I also realized I needed to take charge of the situation, and that meant taking action. So began my systematic search for a new job.

Because the company was not officially "letting me go," it did not offer me paid assistance from an outplacement firm. Instead, I took the initiative myself to seek one out—and even found a firm that was willing to work with me pro bono. Although I'd created my own luck, I felt very lucky to have found the support

---

SUCCESS TIP

Outplacement firms can be helpful in various aspects of your job search, including helping you decide what you are looking for, giving you resources for exploring possible jobs, and connecting you with other people, among other services. If you have been displaced from a job and outplacement services are part of your severance package, take advantage of them.

Remember: whether or not you are working with an outplacement firm, ultimately YOU are the one who must find the job. No one can do it for you!

Once I engaged in the outplacement process, I quickly realized that I needed to treat job hunting as if the search itself were my new job—especially because I was intent on finding a new position within my six-month window.

Treating my search like a job meant that I woke up early every day, dressed in business attire, and either went to the outplacement firm's offices or used my time wisely at home to begin compiling my lists of contacts and making phone calls to schedule meetings with existing or new contacts. Ultimately, I created a daily, weekly, and monthly plan, and I went after finding a new job with a vengeance.

Within six months I did indeed land my dream job. And much to my surprise, my new position took me to Baltimore, Maryland, where I've been living happily ever since.

Creating My Dream Job

Fast-forward to 2008, just before the economy turned bad. Suddenly, my new dream job—the one I'd moved to Maryland to take—turned into a layoff.

With the new job I'd chosen to stay in publishing, and as it happened, the publishing industry was one of the first to experience a surge of layoffs. This was partly because the nature and economics of publishing were changing as the industry moved from print formats to digital, and partly because of the recession's overall influence.

The situation might have seemed like déjà vu—only this time my circumstances were very different. My two children were older now, almost through college, and I had some flexibility I didn't have the previous time. Now I decided that rather than look for another job, it was time to start my own business.

What had changed between the first job loss and this one? I had.

Because the focus of the publishing industry was shifting, I was losing interest in the business—and I realized I was no longer in alignment with either the work or the industry. And I finally realized that my skills, talents, and passions were transferrable.

My passion has always been helping businesses grow and helping people find fulfillment through their work. It was those interests that led me to become a business growth advisor and executive coach.

Planning for Success

At the time I decided to start my own coaching business, my biggest challenge was the limited network of people I knew outside the publishing industry. Although my residence was in Baltimore, I'd traveled extensively for the job that had downsized me, and as a result I knew almost no one in the city. Starting and growing a business requires strong relationships built on trust and respect, and I knew I didn't have many of those at the outset.

I also knew that, in many ways, starting a business is similar to finding a new job:
- You need to believe it's possible.
- You need to get clear about what you want to create and accomplish with the business.
- You need to develop your network and educate people about why you would be a valuable asset for them.

Developing trusted relationships takes time, and I realized that, beyond engaging in persistent, strategic action, there was little I could do to speed up that process and grow the business to a point at which it would support me. What I *could* do was to use the same approach that had served me so well in my first job search: create a targeted action plan, and follow it consistently.

When I launched my new business, I set out with daily, weekly, and monthly plans to develop relationships and build the business—just as I'd done in my previous job search. This time, I attended five to seven networking events a week, and I routinely met one-to-one with 10 to 15 people each week, to get to know as many people as possible, as quickly as possible. I was then able to leverage my new network to help me meet even more new people. Throughout this process, I focused on finding ways to help the people I met—either by connecting them with others who might in some way help them grow their own businesses, or by helping them in a specific area where they were feeling stuck, by offering free advice and coaching.

My Life Today

It's now more than eight years since I started my executive coaching business, and not only am I doing work that I love, I'm also generating more money than I did in my executive position. And the best part is, I'm able to help people every single day to grow their businesses beyond their expectations and help them live more fulfilled lives.

I've included my story here, at the beginning of this book, to show that I'm an example of my own approach. My story illustrates the process. I'm about to show you in the chapters to come.

Over the course of working with many coaching clients, I started noticing some common themes. For example, I saw how people who are unfulfilled or unhappy in their work generally are out of alignment with the job or the company itself (or both), just as I was in 2008 with publishing. In the next chapter I'll help you understand why being in alignment is so important to your future. And in the chapters that follow, I'll revisit some of the other themes from my story in this chapter and show you how you can use the planning and action steps that worked for me to help you succeed in your own job search.

ACTION STEP: JOURNALING

In your journal, explore your answers to these questions:
- What beliefs have kept me from seeking more fulfilling work?
- If money didn't matter, what work would I seek out?

PART I

Understanding Your Beliefs and How They Affect Your Job Search

CHAPTER 2

Alignment and Core Values: How You Are Wired and Why It Matters

Life is not accumulation, it is about contribution.
—Steven Covey

This chapter focuses on the importance of alignment in your work and explores why it's so important to understand alignment during your job search. Its goal is twofold: to help you gain insight about why some of your past jobs didn't work out, and to help you become aligned for future success.

My ultimate vision is that all employees will have jobs in which they are fully aligned with their work and feel fulfilled, and that businesses will thrive as a result.

What Is Alignment?

To understand why alignment is so important, think about your car. A car that's out of alignment rattles and doesn't perform well. The same is true for you in your work life. Just as proper alignment allows your car to run smoothly and efficiently, being in proper alignment with your work allows you to achieve better results and greater success.

Being in alignment means you are doing the work you are meant to be doing—work that is in sync with your core values, that gives you energy, and that allows you to make a contribution in a way that only you can.

The Consequences of Misalignment

In the Preface, I mentioned a Gallup poll result showing that 70% of all workers in the U.S. workforce are disengaged. Why is this statistic so high? Because these workers are out of alignment with their jobs! I see this with clients all the time.

Although some people leave jobs because of layoffs, many leave because they either dislike their work, no longer find their work to be fulfilling or a good fit, disagree with company decisions, or dislike their boss. Others simply don't do well in their jobs, either failing at them outright or experiencing what feels to them like failure. In the long run, a job won't work out if the employee is out of alignment with it.

People who don't do well in a job usually are not bad people—they are simply people who are in the wrong job. While a worker's skills may not be a fit at Company A, he or she might move to Company B and discover that that job is a perfect fit, because it is defined differently.

Aligning With What Motivates You

We all have a desire to make a contribution to the world. The more we focus on the best way to make it, the more successful each of us will be. When you align with what motivates you and engage in work that feels effortless, you will be able to perform your work more effectively and feel fulfilled.

"Effortless work" does not mean work that's not challenging—it means the kind of work that sometimes makes you say to yourself, "People actually pay me to do this!" Think of a job where you were generally excited to go to work every day. How did that affect the quality of your work and your sense of fulfillment?

Even if you've never felt this way about a job, I guarantee that when you find alignment with work that feels effortless—more like fun than work—in a place where the organizational culture is a good fit, you will experience that kind of excitement about your job.

SUCCESS TIP

When seeking a job that plays to your strengths, you should evaluate not only the job itself but also the prospective employer and the organizational culture to determine whether the job and the company are a good "fit" for you.

You'll know when this happens because you'll feel excited about taking the position and will wake up feeling eager to go to work.

Discovering How You Are Wired

Recognizing your own motivations, needs, and purpose is an essential step in understanding how you are aligned and finding a job that feels effortless. But how do you get the information you need? I recommend two tools that I use with my clients to help you in this undertaking: the Core Values Index, and journaling.

The Core Values Index (CVI)

You are a unique recipe of core values and energy. There are no good, bad, right, or wrong core values—you simply are the way you are, and who you are today is how you were wired from birth. The Core Values Index is a tool that helps you understand how you are aligned, what motivates you, and how you are wired. My own experiences in working with clients have shown the CVI to be a great tool for helping properly align people with their work.

I discovered the CVI through Lynn Taylor, a gentleman who spent about 20 years working as a turnaround consultant. At any given time, Lynn was working with eight to 10 companies to "turn them around" from not making money to making a great deal of money—often two to three times their industries' average profit. The primary focus of Lynn's work with those companies was employee alignment.

To better understand how you are wired, take the free CVI at www.susankatzadvantage.com/cvi. Upon completion of the assessment, you will receive a description of your personal core values and gain access to resources written by Lynn Taylor that give you a much deeper understanding of the Core Values Index and your "wired in" nature. If you are interested in a personal coaching session about the Core Values Index, you may also contact me thorugh the same website.

Journaling

A simple way to figure out how you are aligned uses the structured journaling exercise detailed in the Action Step box below. Completing it takes two to four weeks.

I did this exercise myself before leaving my publishing career, when I was considering starting a business. Over the course of the exercise, I noticed that I always felt greatly energized by meeting with members of my staff to coach them on how to approach various situations. In contrast, I noticed that my energy felt drained when I was required to attend long meetings that had no outcomes.

ACTION STEP: JOURNALING

For this journal exercise, you will spend a minimum of two weeks tracking your responses to various events in your workdays, in list form. At the end of the tracking period, you will review your lists to determine what patterns have emerged.

Choose two facing pages in your journal. Label one page "Energizing Activities," and the other, "De-Energizing Activities." As you proceed through your days, do the following:

- Energizing Activities: List any workday activities that give you energy when you engage in them.
- De-Energizing Activities: List any workday activities that drain your energy on this page.

Some of your workday activities will be neutral, and there's no need to include those. Focus only on the activities that either energize or de-energize you, jotting them down as the events occur.

Keep your list entries simple: avoid judgments, and simply record the activities as they occur.

After two weeks you might feel that you have accumulated sufficient data. However, if you sense that a clear pattern has not yet emerged, or you prefer to have more robust lists on which to base your conclusions, consider extending your tracking period to three weeks or even four.

At the end of your tracking period, review your two lists to determine what patterns have emerged. Then, calculate the percentage of activities in each category, noticing whether most of your work activities fall into one category or the other, or whether they are about evenly divided. If 70 to 80 percent of your activities are in the "de-energize" category, then you are very likely misaligned with your work.

Whether you complete the journal exercise, take the CVI assessment, or do both, taking advantage of the available tools to help you determine your alignment is a critical step toward gaining clarity and finding your dream job.

Achieving Success

Remember, success means different things to different people. It can mean having great personal relationships, feeling fulfilled at work, achieving some level of financial success, or attaining any other goal that represents success for that particular individual. There is no single definition of success—what matters is how you define it for yourself.

WORKSHEETS for THIS CHAPTER

See the Appendix at the back of this book for the following additional material(s) to help you work through this chapter's contents:

Worksheet 1: Strengths

Worksheet 2: Energizing & De-energizing Activities

CHAPTER 3

Clarity: Figuring Out What You Really Want to Do

In this chapter, you'll learn why it's important to look for what you want to do, rather than just look for a job. You'll also learn ways to uncover why you are stuck and how you got that way, continue figuring out what energizes and de-energizes you, and clarify your thoughts so you can clearly communicate your goals and desires to those who can help you find your dream job.

When you are seeking a new job, clarity is a critically important part of the process. It will be challenging to move in a purposeful direction until you're clear about what you want and what type of work you're targeting.

What Is Clarity?

Clarity is freedom from ambiguity—the quality of being clear. Clients told me so often that they walk away from our work together with so much clarity that it made me wonder, why is clarity so important?

When you gain clarity, it becomes much easier to develop a plan of action and stay focused on carrying it out. Think of how it is to drive through thick fog: you can't see very far in front of you, and you worry that you might veer off the road or miss an exit.

You spend extra energy paying attention to where you are going, and it's often stressful. Once the fog clears and the sun is shining, you return to driving effortlessly, you see road signs and exits far in advance, and you feel better because the driving is less stressful. Gaining clarity about your job search is similar.

When I was searching for my new job, I continually felt frustrated that I wasn't finding meaningful and viable work. The actions I took, such as speaking with people to help me identify a job, ultimately helped me gain clarity, but it wasn't until I got even clearer and made the decision to stay in publishing that I quickly found the new job. Because I was so clear and had made a decision with specificity, it was much easier to target prospective employers and communicate my interests to them during our conversations.

Having clarity allows you to focus. Being clear about where you are going lets you recognize opportunities and possibilities that you would not see if you weren't clear about your direction. If you are clear about the type of work you want to be doing, it will be much easier to communicate that information to people who will be able to help you find a job.

Perception Matters

If you look up *clarity* in the dictionary, you'll find a definition similar to this: "clearness or lucidity as to perception or understanding; freedom from indistinctness or ambiguity, the state of being clear or transparent." To me, the key to this definition is the term *perception*—understanding gained by applying the powers of your own mind to gain awareness. Stated another way, gaining clarity is an intentional act that involves decision.

Most of us wish that clarity would just happen on its own. That was something I always wished—that someone would just tell me what type of work I should be doing. But clarity is something you create for yourself, through your own perceptions. No one else can or will define your goals or aspirations for you; that requires conscious effort and focus. It's also important to understand that gaining clarity may take time. The goal of the exercises and information in this book is to help you gain greater clarity, more quickly.

A lack of clarity inevitably leads to confusion. For instance, if a client asks me to make referrals, and she is not clear about what she wants me to do, it's going to be hard for me to make introductions to people who might be able to help her.

On the other hand, when you are clear about what you want and where you're going, you will see opportunities and possibilities that you didn't see before. For example: in passing, someone might make a work-related comment that triggers you to ask more questions or to ask for a referral—something you might not have done if you were unclear. Having clarity will enable you to communicate to others what you are looking to achieve, and they in turn will then be able to help you find your dream job.

Ways to Gain Clarity

If you want clarity, you must treat the pursuit of it seriously, taking 100% responsibility for it! I assume that's why you are reading this book: because you are willing to take complete responsibility for your career. Following are a few techniques I suggest to help my clients gain clarity about what they want.

Recall and Examine a Past Moment of Clarity

Your level of clarity will vary at different times in your life. At some points, you'll be very clear about your future, whereas at other times, probably right now, you'll be unclear. And when that happens, you'll want to take a look back at a time when you had clarity, to examine what you were thinking and how you were feeling.

For instance, I started my publishing career in sales. I remember sitting at my first sales meeting, listening to the company's president speaking to the entire sales organization, and I thought to myself, "I could do that." At that moment, I felt an instant clarity that I was going to move ahead in the firm. I saw and felt very clearly that I was capable of moving forward in the company.

Drill Down for Details

Clarity may occur in an instant, as it did for me at the sales meeting, or it may happen slowly as a result of deep thought, interactions with other people, or engaging in some of the exercises in this book.

Recently I was helping someone who is unemployed. She mentioned that she was looking for a job in project management. While project management may appear to be a specific job goal, it is still fairly vague. Automatically I thought to myself, "What type of project management, and in what industry?" I advised her to spend some time getting more specific about her goal. The next time I saw her, she mentioned that she was interested in doing project management within an advertising agency. As soon as she narrowed her scope and focus, it became much easier for me to make introductions for her to potential employers, or to contacts who might know of prospective employers.

In another example, I was working with a young woman who was in a teaching career she found unfulfilling. Through the course of our conversation, she realized that although she was passionate about education, teaching was not her calling. By gaining clarity about her strengths and how she wanted to spend her time (and on what activities she wanted to focus), she was able to network her way into her dream job as manager of talent at a private graduate school of education that was focused on recruiting strategy and marketing.

So if you have some idea of what you would like to be doing, keep asking yourself questions that will drill down for greater detail. For instance, if you were to decide you really want a job in sports management (a very general goal), you might ask yourself questions such as these:

- What specific job or jobs would I like to do in sports management?
- With whom, or with what companies, would I like to do this work?

Although creating such specificity may seem counterintuitive and feel as if you are ruling out possible opportunities, it will help you communicate a clear message about your future when you are talking with contacts, and it will allow you to target companies or individuals who either have job openings or who are connected to others who might have them.

Visualize the Future

Another way to gain clarity is to visualize the future. One of the best examples I have read about the importance of visualization is in Dana Wilde's book *Train Your Brain*, in which the author shares the results of a research study designed to measure the impact of visualization on performance.

The study began with three groups of people who each took turns throwing a basketball into a hoop, while researchers recorded the results to establish a baseline of each person's shooting accuracy. Then, the first group was told to practice throwing a basketball into a hoop for an hour every day for the next 30 days. The second group was told not to practice but to visualize shooting the basketball into the hoop for an hour every day. The third group was told to do nothing.

When the three groups came back 30 days later and the researchers had them repeat the process, the first group (the ones who had actually practiced) had improved by 23%. The second group (the participants who only visualized shooting the ball) also had improved by 23%. The group whose participants had done nothing showed no improvement.

I mention this story because it illustrates how critically important it is to spend time visualizing the desired results in your future and what they will look like. We so often don't do this, getting stuck in our fear of how we are going to make things happen rather than focusing on what we intend to make happen. Following is an exercise I recommend that you do.

ACTION STEP: VISUALIZATION and JOURNALING
Visualization.

Spend 10 to 15 minutes every day doing the following visualization.

Relax, close your eyes, and imagine in vivid detail your desired future job or business. Notice:
- how you feel when you get up to go to work in the morning.
- the kinds of activities you are engaged in each day.
- the aspects of the job that make you feel energized.
- the people with whom you are working.
- the way you feel when you interact with your colleagues.

If thoughts of worry surface about how to get there, simply release them, and return to visualizing in detail what your job is like, how it feels to have it, and what's going on around you.

Journaling.

As a follow-up to your visualization, jot down notes about the things you noticed or felt. Record as many specific details as you can recall. This will help you start building a roadmap to get you where you want to go. (See also the list of additional Worksheets at the end of this chapter.)

Goals: Why They Matter and How to Work With Them

Here I will devote some detailed attention to goals, because they are so essential to gaining clarity. Setting goals is important, and so are the additional steps of writing them down and then working with them intentionally.

Following is a process I recommend to my clients.

Go Ahead—Set Some Goals!

Most of us are afraid to create goals. We worry that the goals we set won't be the "right" ones, or that we might not achieve them. So, rather than risk "making a mistake," we avoid setting goals at all. Accept that you will make mistakes along the way—and remember, any goal is better than no goal.

Goals can be as simple as committing to meet with five people in a month to help you further your career search, or as big as finding a job that takes you traveling the world.

As you start working with goals, it's a good idea to limit the number you set. You want to set yourself up for success, and creating too many goals will probably leave you feeling scattered and overwhelmed, or even defeated. As my husband likes to say, if you chase too many rabbits at one time, you won't catch any of them.

Begin by creating one to three goals, and add more only after you've completed the initial set.

Put Your Goals in Writing

Once you've decided what your goals are, write them down! If the thought of doing that makes you uncomfortable, you should know that it took me a long time to accept the idea myself. Putting goals down in writing is one of the keys to success, yet few people do it. Both big and small goals are both good, as long as they are specific—more about that below.

You might wonder why putting your goals in writing matters. Isn't it enough simply to know what your goals are? No, and here's one reason why: if a thought stays only in your head, it typically remains there and won't become a reality. Writing down your goals is the first, very important step to making them clear and making them happen.

Create Small, Manageable Steps

Next, break each goal down into smaller steps that represent the associated actions necessary to move you toward your overall goal. I recommend this approach because even small steps, taken consistently, can lead to big results. Keeping your goals small and manageable also makes it much more likely that you will accomplish them, because making a daily choice to do something small is much easier than making a choice to do something big.

For example: if you set a goal to do pushups every day and you've never done them before, it's much easier to do five pushups a day for a month than it is to do 50, and you're also much more likely to accomplish your goal. By the same token, if you're just starting a savings plan, it's easier to start by saving $10 or $20 a week than it is to save $500 a week.

The key here is to take these small steps consistently. Then, as your small actions turn into habits, you can increase the magnitude of the action—for example, re-set your goal and aim for 10 pushups a day, or target saving $40 per week.

Be Specific

Make sure the goals you've written down are specific. A *specific* goal is one you can measure—and that's important, because the ability to measure allows you to know when you've achieved a goal. Notice the difference between these two examples:

> *Nonspecific goal*: Do exercises to strengthen my upper body.
> *Specific goal*: Do five pushups every day for one month.

Go back and re-read the goals you've written down, and make sure they're specific. If any of them are nonspecific, reframe them as in the example above.

Another part of being specific is setting a due date for each goal and its associated action steps. This will help ensure you complete them.

As you implement the actions that will move you toward achieving your goals, your confidence will build. That, in turn, builds positive momentum that ultimately will lead you to some significant results.

Review Your Goals Daily

Once you have written down your goals and broken them into specific, manageable steps, you need to review them daily.

Why is this important? Reviewing something reinforces it in your unconscious mind. Over time, when you take repeated action in support of your goal, the action becomes a habit. Habits are merely behaviors that become automatic—actions you engage in without thinking about them.

Understand Your "Why"

It's important to understand the "why" behind your goals. If a goal is not important to you, then you won't be likely to commit to it or to stay focused on it when you hit a rough patch (and I guarantee you WILL hit some rough patches).

The Core Values Index, mentioned previously, also helps you understand your "why" because it measures how you are motivated. If, for example, you are motivated by being with other people, and you can visualize yourself interacting with others, then your underlying motivation is that interacting with people energizes you. In contrast, you may be someone who likes to sit quietly to figure things out, or you enjoy repetitive work that requires precision. If so, your motivation may be that working quietly on your own energizes you.

ACTION STEP: JOURNALING

Begin by watching the TED talk by Simon Sinek titled *How great leaders inspire action*. Sinek's talk addresses the importance of understanding the "why" behind your behavior, actions, and goals.

Then, review the goals you wrote down. What is it about each goal that matters to you? Ask yourself this question about each one in turn, spending a few minutes exploring the answers in your journal. Be specific. Understanding why a goal matters to you will help sustain you through the challenging times when your motivation flags.

Focus and Persist

It's essential that you stay focused, consistent, and persistent with the actions you take toward your goals. You will undoubtedly have times when you just don't feel like doing something—almost everyone I talk to feels that way some of the time, myself included. But if you've made a commitment to a goal, you're more likely to choose to move forward and take the necessary action.

There have been numerous times in my own life when I've thought, "I'm bagging this... it just feels too hard." But ultimately I persisted, because I'd made a commitment to accomplish the goal I'd created. A case in point was writing this book. I didn't write it overnight—I allocated a small amount of time every week to work on it, and eventually, I completed it. In general, I'm someone who would rather be out interacting with people or reading someone else's book instead of writing my own. However, I knew that writing the book would allow me to help more people find fulfilling work, and that's part of my mission. So many people have asked me for help with their career transitions that I knew the book needed to be completed.

Remember not only to stay focused on your goals, but also to have patience with yourself as you work toward them. Finding your ideal job may take time. It will certainly take consistent effort, and you need to believe that it's possible.

* * * * *

Overall, gaining clarity relies on your ability to determine what energizes you and to understand and align with your strengths. If you don't spend the time necessary to figure it out, it won't happen. No one else can do it for you.

In conclusion, I leave you with this example about clarity. I was at a networking event, and one of the people in the group told us he was a consultant. Because I enjoy connecting people with each other, I kept asking him questions. But no matter how many questions I asked to help him clarify what he does, he couldn't provide a clear answer. Without good information from him, I was unable to help make connections for him.

Similarly, if you don't have clarity, it will be hard for others to help you. And remember, others WILL help you, once you are able to communicate clearly to them what you want to do.

WORKSHEETS for THIS CHAPTER

See the Appendix at the back of this book for the following additional material(s) to help you work through this chapter's contents:

Worksheet 3: A Day At Your Dream Job

CHAPTER 4

Mindset, Belief, Behavior: What They Are and Why They Matter

When I was in grade school, I spent years thinking of myself as a terrible athlete. I was always one of the last to be chosen for the kickball team, and my friends made fun of me because I couldn't figure out how to climb a tree. As other incidents of this sort happened, they fed my growing "I'm a terrible athlete" belief, becoming part of the story I told myself about who I was—a story I'd cobbled together from other people's opinions. Any time I wasn't chosen for a team, any time I couldn't perform an athletic task, there was one more bit of evidence I used to support my belief.

I continued to allow others' opinions of me to shape my opinion of myself, until one day I consciously decided to change my view of myself. I realized I'd been treating others' opinions as fact and that there were probably many athletic pursuits I could do well. Subsequently, I became an excellent swimmer (I even went on to perform water ballet), learned to scuba dive, learned to rock climb, and actively participated in fitness classes at the gym. In fact, I've been involved in athletic pursuits of one kind or another ever since.

I share this story here because it illustrates how mindset and belief can influence behavior, both for worse and for better.

Because mindset, belief, and behavior are all so important to your future success in landing your dream job, I believe it's critically important for you to gain awareness of what habitual, automatic, limiting beliefs might be holding you back from achieving success. This chapter and the next are both devoted to helping you understand your mindset and beliefs, your story, and the ways in which your story has been affecting your search for a job.

Mindset

What is mindset, and how does it differ from belief? As defined in the dictionary, mindset is a fixed mental attitude or disposition that predetermines a person's responses to and interpretations of situations—that is, it's an inclination or habit of mind. What's most important to note about this definition is the word predetermine: to decide in advance how to respond to or approach a situation. So, if you have predetermined that it's going to be difficult to find a job, I guarantee that it will be difficult.

In her book *Mindset: The New Psychology of Success*, author Carol Dweck talks about two kinds of mindset: growth mindset and fixed mindset. With a growth mindset, people view mistakes or ineffective actions as opportunities to learn. In contrast, fixed-mindset people believe they are born with skills and talents that cannot be changed, therefore they fear making mistakes and view mistakes as failure.

What is your mindset? Take a moment to consider your own perceptions and the habitual ways in which you tend to interpret and respond to situations. Are you more of a fixed-mindset person, or a growth-mindset person? If you discover that your mindset is more fixed, and you're tired of looking for a job, burned out on job interviews that seem to go nowhere, and frustrated that the job search seems to be more work than it's worth, that can all change now. This is your book, and its only mission is to get you focused—on gaining clarity, changing your behavior, creating a realistic and positive mindset, and developing a plan of action. You *can* change your own mindset—I did. Consider the story I just shared.

Mindset often leads to belief. For example: if you have predetermined (decided in advance) that finding your dream job is possible, then it will become much easier to accomplish because you accept that it's true.

Belief

Belief is defined as something one accepts as true or real—a firmly held opinion or conviction. Our beliefs develop from our past experiences and are stored in our unconscious mind. Many of our beliefs are formed by the time we turn six years old. The people who surround us as we are growing up give us their opinions, and we begin to accept those opinions as our own truth.

Belief strongly influences our behavior. For example:
- If you are of the opinion (have a conviction) that you will find a great job, then you will eventually make it happen—because belief will cause you to take different actions from those you would have taken if you didn't believe it was possible to find a great job.
- If you believe you'll retire comfortably and are committed to doing so, then you'll begin to take the necessary actions to start saving money consistently for retirement or planning how you will spend your retirement.
- If you believe you're healthy and active, then you will behave accordingly by exercising and eating the right food.

Belief is why a fixed mindset can change—because you can change what you believe. It starts with a shift in perception.

Consider again the example of what I believed as a child about my athletic abilities. Once I made the decision to change my view of myself and chose a different belief, I began to perceive myself differently. I then perceived new possibilities that I wouldn't have seen otherwise. My new belief had opened my mind to the presence of athletic activities I could do well and enjoy. What had happened was that I'd supported my decision with new data: I began looking for athletic activities I could do successfully, and then the act of doing them further reinforced my new belief.

We all do this unconsciously and unquestioningly. In fact, up to 95% of our behaviors and beliefs are habitual or unconscious—which means we engage in those habits, behaviors, and beliefs automatically without ever thinking about them. What a tremendous opportunity for change this represents!

Behavior

A positive belief can take you far. The story I shared earlier about my first sales meeting, when I watched the company president while thinking to myself that I would one day move into executive management—well, that belief led me onto a path of learning how people advanced within the company. By taking the appropriate actions and doing my job in a way that added value to the company, I then gradually worked my way up the corporate ladder. And it all started in my imagination, where I laid down the path for myself.

Throughout my career, I continued believing that career advancement was possible. All the while, I made sure I did each job assigned to me as well as possible, because I wanted to be recognized as a valuable player. No advancement or achievement happens simply by imagining it. It's always necessary to take the appropriate actions and look for ways to add value in the organization.

Had I not held the belief that I could move into executive management, I might have switched to a different career or stayed on the sales team. I want to be clear that there's no right or wrong position in a company—staying in sales would have been a great alternative (I happen to love selling). But the fact is, somewhere inside myself I believed I could challenge myself in other ways, and because I believed it was possible, I chose a different path.

Advancing into executive management within an organization was new ground for me. My mother was a secretary in the police department in the town where I grew up, and my father was in window and siding sales. Neither had gone to college. I grew up believing I would become a nurse, a social worker, or a teacher—all of which are great jobs, but not a fit for me. If I had pursued any of those positions, I likely would have failed.

Even though I had no role models in my immediate family for the type of position I was pursuing, I did receive encouragement to do whatever kind of work I chose. My mother and father believed in me, and subsequently, I chose to believe (saw possibilities) in myself. I eventually rose to the level of vice-president, a position in which I had considerable responsibility for profit, loss, and the performance of the teams who worked for me.

What you believe WILL determine your level of success.

So will your ability to focus. As you've already read in previous chapters, focus is critical to both individual and organizational success. If everything is equally important, then nothing is important, and eventually you get lost in the "spin" of ideas. You end up feeling paralyzed and unable to take the actions needed to help you reach your goals. But with clarity and focus, you'll be able to break down your action plan into small, manageable steps, prioritizing which actions are most important to take first.

Taking those small steps will help build both your confidence and your momentum toward your goals. Remember, small steps taken consistently and persistently will lead to big results.

Persistent Action

I can't stress enough the importance of consistent, persistent action taken over a period of time. We've become a society of "instant" results, and we often forget that the most successful people have consistently and persistently pursued their goals. They didn't necessarily know how they were going to achieve those results, but they did have some things in common. All of them:
- had belief.
- could envision a positive future.
- focused on doing the right activities to help them reach their goals.
- were able to learn from mistakes (had growth mindset).
- consistently took actions that moved them forward.

Successful people do "fail" along the way—but they use their failures as opportunities to learn what to differently in the future. Failure is merely practice. Engaging in a new behavior after making a mistake and continuing to practice the successful behavior rapidly builds new neural pathways in the brain. The new behavior eventually will become automatic and will start to occur unconsciously.

Remember, you didn't learn to walk the first time you stood up, and you didn't learn to drive a car the first time you got behind the wheel. And, you wouldn't have learned to drive a car if all you'd done was learn about driving and not practice the actions that make it happen.

Similarly, you won't find a new job the first time you go out and work your network. I didn't find a new job or build my business after the first, second, or even third conversations—it took many conversations and much persistent behavior before I succeeded in those pursuits. It also took belief that eventually I would reach my goal—otherwise I would never have taken the necessary actions to get there, nor would I have persisted when the going got tough. I treated job hunting like a contact sport: I practiced contacting enough people to grow the network that ultimately helped me find my dream job. I recommend that you do the same!

CHAPTER 5

Your Story: Understanding How Your Past Has Been Shaping Your Future

When I was starting my business, one of the most powerful books I read was Jim Loehr's *The Power of Story: Change Your Story, Change Your Destiny in Business and in Life.* Loehr's premise is that we carry personal stories about ourselves in our heads that have been shaped by our past, and those stories continue to shape our future. If you are able to change your story, then you will be able to change your future. Loehr gives many great examples of people to whom that has happened.

As I read Loehr's book, I realized that one of the limiting stories I carried about myself came from something that happened when I was eight years old. I was sitting with a group of family members and friends. One of the adults asked my opinion about a political topic of which I had no knowledge, and I didn't have an answer. I remember feeling embarrassed, and for a long time afterward I was afraid to state my opinion in a group of people. I've mostly overcome that fear, but it comes up every once in a while when I'm with a group of people I don't know well.

Shawn Achor, a well-known Harvard professor with a popular TED talk on YouTube, writes about alternate realities in his book *Before Happiness.* Achor says there is no "right" reality—that is, two different people can have two very different perceptions of the same situation (two different stories). I experienced this first-hand when I took a friend with me to a unique, high-intensity strength training workout I do every Saturday.

As my friend, Andrea, and I were speaking with the owner of the fitness facility, he was explaining how and why the exercise program is so effective. After the workout, when Andrea and I discussed the conversation over coffee, she shared with me that she initially had thought the owner came across as arrogant and cocky. I, on the other hand, had thought he came across as passionate and knowledgeable about his subject. There we were—two people who had listened to the same conversation, in the same room, yet came away with two completely different interpretations. Neither interpretation was right or wrong—each was simply a result of our preexisting beliefs and life experiences. If other people had been with us, we likely would have heard several other reactions.

Choosing a different reality sounds like a simple concept, yet it takes conscious, ongoing effort to bring about change. Since it's possible to choose your reality, why not choose one that serves you in a positive way, by focusing on what is possible, rather than one that limits you by focusing on what you believe is not possible?

Thoughts and Beliefs That Hold Us Back

It is part of our human survival instinct to focus on what is negative or perceived as negative. According to Shad Helmstetter, in his book What to Say When You Talk to Yourself, leading behavioral researchers report that as much as 77 percent of our thought content is negative and counterproductive, working against us. If we grew up in an average home, during the first 18 years of our lives we were told "no"—what we could not do—more than 148,000 times. During that same time, we were told "yes," or what we could do, only a few hundred times, perhaps a thousand at most. Is it any wonder, then, that most of us focus on what's NOT possible rather than what IS? (Perhaps this helps explain the popularity of the children's book The Little Engine That Could!)

Some of the limiting statements and beliefs I've heard from people about work are these:
- I'm too old—no one will want to hire me.
- I don't have enough experience to be hired in my field.
- The economy is so bad it's impossible to find a new job.
- I don't have skills that anyone will want.
- All the good jobs are taken.
- I've sent out hundreds of resumes and no one ever responds.
- It's the holidays, and no one does business at the end of the year.

Do any of these statements sound familiar? If they do, I guarantee that whether you are aware of it or not, you are projecting these beliefs when you interact with people. Each of these statements is self-defeating, limiting, and lacking in personal accountability. They are all examples of limiting beliefs: decisions we make about ourselves that limit our lives and prevent us from taking positive action.

If you spend your time blaming external circumstances and don't take responsibility for making different choices in your beliefs and your behavior, you will keep getting what you've been getting—nothing!

Overcoming Limiting Beliefs

We all go through times of negative thinking—it's what you choose to do with the negative thoughts that will help you change your results. Here's an example from my own experience.

> Three weeks into my new business, a networking colleague told me no one would ever hire me—not because he didn't like me, but because he didn't believe in what I did for a living.

If I'd listened to my colleague, I would have stopped trying and would not be in this business today. Instead, I chose to form my own opinions about my business, because I believed I had something to offer others that would help them significantly. This isn't to say I didn't experience any limiting beliefs along the way—I did, as we all do. I sometimes encounter them now, even though I've built a successful business. The key is to take steps to transform them.

❧ Step 1: Become Aware of the Limiting Belief

The first step to overcoming the limiting beliefs that sabotage you along the way is to identify, or gain awareness of, them. Another personal example will serve here.

> I had a strong limiting belief that kept me from public speaking for almost a year. Although I had done a great deal of presenting in my corporate career, when I started my business, I felt inadequate to speak in public. I didn't think I was knowledgeable enough to give advice to a room full of people, and I was worried that people might judge me as "stupid." I thought to myself, "What do I have to say that could be valuable to other people?" When I thought about how people might judge me, I felt fearful and scared.
>
> The limiting belief underlying my self talk was, I'm not good enough to offer advice to others.

Public speaking is one of the ways I get new clients. By allowing my limiting belief to rule my behavior, I didn't take appropriate actions and thus limited the number of speaking opportunities

I sought out. My belief influenced my actions and, ultimately, my results—meaning fewer prospective clients.

Step 2: Reframe Your Thinking

Once you've identified that you are operating from a limiting belief, the next step is to reframe your thinking. Here are some examples from the preceding section of how the limiting beliefs about finding work might be reframed:

> I have great skills that will be of considerable value to an organization.
>
> There are many companies and job opportunities.
>
> I have a network of people who want to help me find a job that's a fit for me.
>
> Companies are seeking people with my years of experience.
>
> Employers have more time to review resumes during the quieter time of the holiday season.

Step 3: Set Incremental, Achievable Goals

Returning to my public speaking example, once I'd identified the negative belief behind my behavior, I decided that I wanted to overcome it, because it was limiting my results. I worked with my coach, Greg (yes, even coaches use coaches to help them reach new levels of success), to map out a plan.

I had just heard Ron Shapiro, the well-known sports agent and negotiator, speak. I told Greg that although I thought I was a good speaker, I wanted to be "great" like Ron Shapiro. I also shared that in my past speaking engagements, I hadn't gotten the results I expected. I told Greg I was frustrated that people were not "flocking" to me after I spoke, asking me to work with them!

Together, Greg and I worked out a plan:

- First, Greg challenged me to rethink my approach by breaking it down into more manageable steps. He suggested that, rather than aim to be "great," I aim to go from "good" to "better." Great advice.
- He asked if I believed I added value when I worked with clients in a one-to-one setting. His question not only helped me realize that I absolutely did believe I added value in that setting but also spurred me to rethink that limiting belief.
- Greg worked with me around my expectations regarding the results of my speaking engagements. He helped me become aware that I was far too attached to the outcome and suggested that, rather than worry about how many clients I generated from the engagements, I focus instead on adding value.
- Finally, Greg suggested that I think of the audience to whom I was speaking as one person, and that I focus on their needs rather than my own needs.

I set a one-year goal of 12 speaking engagements—one a month. I broke that goal down further into specific actions that I would take over the next 30 days:

1. I would secure a speaking engagement with an audience that was NOT in my target market. I chose this audience to reduce my attachment to the outcome and my stress level. I viewed it as practice.
2. I read the book Trust Me by Nick Morgan, a well-known speaking coach.

3. I practiced my new speech with my son, who always provides good, honest feedback.

The result of this plan was that I secured a speaking engagement with a group of administrative professionals. The speech went so well that one of the participants approached me at the end of my talk to tell me that I had changed her life. Her husband had recently passed away, and she felt stuck in a cycle of going home every evening after work and feeling sad and depressed. As a result of my talk, she was able to see how she could break that pattern and create something new for herself. Greg had said I should focus on adding value for the participants, and I thought to myself, "Boy, did I achieve that!" That feeling was better than any new clients I might have generated from the talk. Interestingly enough, a year later the regional chapter of this same administrative professionals group paid me to come and speak at their meeting. By focusing on adding value, I ended up generating business.

It's important here to clarify the difference between being intentional and being attached to outcome. An intention is an aim or purpose that guides your actions. For example, writing down your goals as described in earlier chapters and being intentional about achieving them makes it much more likely that you will achieve your desired end. In contrast, being "attached" to an outcome means you've decided you must have that particular outcome. Attaching your happiness or success to specific outcomes often causes stress.

In the case of my public speaking engagements, if I had maintained my initial attachment to a particular outcome, I would have been disappointed every time I didn't get clients from a speaking engagement. Instead, I focused on how much value I was able to offer the participants and how I gave them an opportunity to engage with me after the speaking engagement.

Although I advise that you avoid attachment to outcome, I'm not saying you should be passive about your goals. I believe it's important to be as proactive as possible about achieving your goals, while focusing on the areas you can control—and you cannot control outcomes. You can only influence them through your actions. Your focus should be on the steps you take and what you learn as you take them, because those are the only things within your control. Being present to the process and your actions will provide you with the greatest sense of fulfillment, happiness, and success.

❧ Step 4: Plan For Future Improvement

It's always important to have a "Plan B" for those times when things don't go as intended and your actions miss the mark.

When great athletes don't succeed, they don't blame circumstances—instead, they examine what they need to do differently next time (this is the growth mindset). They also plan for what to do if circumstances themselves are less than ideal. For example, the great Olympic swimmer Michael Phelps planned what he would do if his goggles ever fell off while he was swimming—so when the situation actually occurred, he was prepared and knew how to handle it.

❧ Step 5: Create An Empowering Belief to Live By

The final step in overcoming a limiting belief is to create an empowering belief by which you will live. An empowering belief is one that is based on the future rather than the past and that encourages us to believe in ourselves. Empowering beliefs enable us to achieve our dreams and goals. For public speaking, my empowering belief was this:

When I speak publicly, I have a positive impact on people, leaving them feeling energized, hopeful, and able to see new opportunities for success.

Creating an empowering belief is a choice! But how do you "flip the switch" to go from a limiting belief to an empowering belief?

Actors sometimes use a technique called "anchoring": finding a particular thought that will evoke a particular emotion on cue, and then calling forth that thought when they need to express that emotion. The technique I recommend is similar, and I like to refer to the thought as a "trigger"—because the thought will trigger your empowering belief.

The technique is this:
- Because thoughts are the precursors to emotions (you can't experience an emotion without having had an associated thought first), you need to identify a very specific trigger thought that leaves you feeling positive. The thought might be one of a past experience in which you looked for a job and had a great conversation with a person who was helpful. Or it might be an experience from another area of your life that left you feeling empowered.
- Then, whenever you become aware that you are experiencing your limiting belief, immediately substitute the trigger thought you created. (Your mind allows you to have only one thought at a time, so why not choose one that's empowering?)
- Once your trigger thought has evoked your positive feelings, you can remind yourself of your empowering belief.

The following activity provides specific steps to help you "flip the switch" in this way.

ACTION STEP: JOURNALING

What are your limiting beliefs?

First, list as many of your limiting beliefs as you can think of. Then, for each limiting belief, write down an empowering belief to counteract it.

Now, go through your list and decide on one of these empowering beliefs to be your focus as you go through your job search.

Write the empowering belief you selected on 5 to 10 sticky notes, and place them throughout your home. Practice thinking and saying aloud your empowering belief 10 times in the morning, 10 times in the middle of the day, and 10 times at night.

In my case, since I hadn't had a great deal of experience with speaking events where I'd felt empowered, I chose as my trigger thought the memory of when my husband, Jim, and I were married in Las Vegas by an Elvis impersonator. Whenever I thought about that, I smiled and felt happy. That trigger thought allowed me to relax and focus on the audience rather than myself, and it also reminded me to think about the empowering belief I'd created.

I remember one talk in particular, where I presented to a hundred people. As I was walking to the room, I became aware that I was moving into negative self-talk. Immediately, I chose to think about our wedding. That put me in such a positive frame of mind that I couldn't help but smile, and I received great feedback on the talk that day. I left the presentation feeling as if I'd "nailed" it!

Now that you understand the importance of mindset and belief, and you have identified an empowering belief to focus on through your job search, we'll consider how to build your social network.

The remainder of this book focuses on practical ways to help get you into action to meet people, make connections, and find your dream job.

PART 2

Creating an Action Plan for Your Job Search

CHAPTER 6

Building A Social Network that Works for You: Finding and Meeting the People in Your Network

A question people frequently ask me is, "How do I find the right connections?"

Of the many possible answers, I want to focus here on two. One answer is that you should target people who you believe might be able to help you as you search for your new position. However, you won't always know in advance who those people are. This leads to the second answer, which is that you should avoid ruling anyone out, especially at the beginning of your search, because you don't know who they might know.

When I was searching for an executive-level position in publishing, I preferred to meet and speak with people who hired people for the level of position I was seeking—that is, anyone who would be hiring at the vice president level in higher education publishing. However, everyone has connections, and sometimes a person who seems to be totally unrelated to your job search will either have a connection to someone who can help, or be able to connect you with someone in your target area of interest.

My best response to the question above, then, is this: When you start networking to find a job, cast a wide net. Think of it as "opening the water faucets all the way." Then, as your search goes on, you can gradually "slow the flow" as you become more discerning about the network connections you make.

Two Types of Networking

The intention behind business networking as I coach it is to have your existing network of people—those you already know—cast their nets out to others in their own networks: others you might not yet know but who might be able to help you in your job search. In this way, you expand your reach.

I like to distinguish between two kinds of networking: the kind done at networking events, and the kind that happens in one-to-one networking conversations:

> *Conversations at networking events* typically generate leads. At these events, it's not in your best interest to "sell" yourself but instead to focus on identifying one, two, or three people who might be a good resource for you in your job search. These conversations tend to be quick. They are not necessarily (or even typically) held with people who have open positions in their companies, but rather people who might be able to help connect you with others who do. These people could be in a similar industry to yours, or could know people in that industry. They could also be people who appear to be good connectors.
>
> *One-to-one networking conversations*, in contrast, are your opportunity to follow up on the leads you've gotten, whether through networking events or personal referrals. Whereas your focus at a networking event is generating leads, your goal in a one-to-one networking conversation is *relationship building*. The conversation is more in-depth, and it may happen either

by phone or in person over coffee or lunch. In either case, it's an opportunity for you to learn more about the person with whom you're meeting and find out if there are ways you might be able to help each other.

Networking: What It Isn't, and What It Is

Networking is NOT a linear activity—in other words, when you meet someone, that person may not lead you to your next job interview, but he or she may very well lead you to someone, who will lead you to someone else, who will then lead you to yet one more person, who eventually will lead you to the person with the job. In the end, there may be many human links (connections) between you and the person with the open position. This is a perfect illustration of the phrase "six degrees of separation," often attributed to the actor Kevin Bacon.

The theory of six degrees of separation was originally proposed by Frigyes Karinthy. It holds that everyone is six or fewer steps away, by way of introduction, from any other person in the world. In this way, a chain of "a friend of a friend" statements theoretically can be made to connect any two people in a maximum of six steps (*Wikipedia*).

Networking may not be linear, but it IS a web of connections, similar in form and function to a spider web. A spider weaves a web to serve as an efficient way to catch its prey (insects) without having to run the prey down. In much the same way, you will be creating a web to "catch" potential jobs without randomly applying at companies where you have no warm connections or endorsements from friends. Just as constructing the web requires the spider to expend energy, so will you have to expend energy to create the "web" of contacts that will ultimately help you catch your dream job. The key is to be in action consistently, adding people continually to your web.

Getting in Front of the Right People

To expand your network, it is important to qualify and get in front of as many of the right people as possible. Again, don't worry about whether each person is the "right" person. If you speak with enough people, you will eventually get in front of more of the "right" people. Sometimes networking will feel like dating, where only one out of many will be a good fit for you. Remember, a job search is a numbers game. The more people you engage with, the more likely you will be to find the person within a company that is looking for someone just like you.

Many of the people you will meet won't have a job available at the time you meet them. But when a position in their company does open up, you will have established enough of a relationship that you can circle back to that person to help get you introduced to the hiring manager or human resources person. That will be a much more powerful approach than having your resume land undistinguished alongside hundreds of other resumes.

It may seem counterintuitive, but looking for "THE" job when you're starting your search actually may be counterproductive. If you discover a job lead that appears to be a good fit for you, then by all means, inquire about it and pursue it. In general, though, you will be much more likely to land an interview if you find someone to introduce you into the company and, even better, to the people who will be doing the hiring and interviewing.

Even when you find a desirable open position on a job board that you plan to apply for, it's still helpful to find someone in your network who might be able to introduce you into the company before you apply. Your contact will be more likely to steer you in the right direction and, ideally, will be able to make a warm introduction to help move your name and resume to the top of the pile.

Developing Your Network

I hope by now you're convinced that the best way to find a job is through personal contacts. If you're still wavering, consider this: everyone you know has at least 250 contacts and, thanks to social media, likely many more than that.

The best way to start developing your network is to write down a list of everyone you know in your life—including every area. Follow these steps:

1. Create as long a list of your contacts (your "natural network") as possible. Don't worry about whether or not each person is the "right" type of person.
2. Make a list of companies you would like to work for, so that as you meet with people, you will be able to reference the list to ask for connections into those companies.
3. Set a goal for how many people you will speak with or meet with each week. For example, in my job search during my publishing career, I set a goal of having a minimum of five conversations a week, and at times I had as many as 10.
4. Systematically schedule calls of 20 to 30 minutes, coffee meetings, or office meetings with your contacts to ask for their help. Be sure to keep track of your referrals and the status of your contacts with them.
5. Ask everyone you meet if they would be willing to introduce you to one, two, or three contacts. Specifically saying "one, two, or three contacts" is much more effective than asking someone, "Who do you know?", because it asks people to narrow their thinking. You will be much more likely to walk away with at least one additional contact.

The box at the end of this chapter contains a list of Worksheets designed to help you with the above steps. These worksheets are located in the Appendix at the end of this book.

Identifying qualified people to speak with is easier today than ever, thanks to the strong influence of social media. However, DO NOT contact people to say you are looking for a job and want to find out if they might have one for you. Focus instead on seeking help. Say, "I'm in transition and am looking to change jobs, and I'd like to get your advice about my search." Consider how you feel when someone approaches you and asks for something you might not be able to provide, compared with how you feel when someone asks for your advice. Most people love to give advice and help others.

Following Up

Anytime you interact with someone who has offered to help you, it's a good idea to use permission-based questions as a way to find out how the other person prefers to provide the help. For example, during the course of a conversation, as soon as someone offers to introduce you to a person who might be able to help further your job search, ask, "When would be a good time for me to follow up with you about connecting me to this person? Would you prefer that I follow up with you by email, or by phone?"

When you finally meet with someone or speak with them by phone, always ask the person for his or her business card (if meeting in person) or their postal mailing address (if speaking by phone), so you will have relevant contact information. If someone has taken the time to meet with you, it's important to express your appreciation. And although this may sound old-fashioned, you can never go wrong with a handwritten thank you note. In this age of email and texting, handwritten notes will help you set you apart, because so few people send them.

ACTION STEP: PRACTICE EXERCISE

- Working with your list of contacts (your "natural network"), set a weekly goal for how many people you will call and how many people you will schedule to meet with each week.
- Based upon your weekly goal, begin making calls to schedule phone calls or meetings with the people on your list.
- At the end of each call, be sure to ask for introductions to the one, two, or three people your contact knows who might be able to help you further your job search. Be specific when you ask your contact for the introductions.
- Create a list of the new contacts.
- If you need to follow up with your original contact to find out if the person they recommended is willing to speak or meet with you, note the date for follow up and add it to your calendar.
- Remember to follow up with a thank you note to each person with whom you speak or meet.

Being Specific and Why It Matters

In your networking conversations, specificity is important, in both the questions you ask and your description of the kind of job you want to find. For example, the question "Who do you know?" is broad and open-ended, and it elicits a very different response than does asking, "Who are the one or two people you know?" As to being specific about the type of job you are seeking, another example will illustrate. When I started my job search in publishing and was unclear whether I would stay in publishing, I wasn't able to expand my network effectively. As soon as I gained clarity, got specific, and decided what I wanted to do (which was to continue as a vice president for an educational publishing company), I started getting great leads.

You will continually expand your network by asking each person you meet who are the one, two, or three people they know who might be able to help you in your job search. When you ask for introductions, remember to be specific about the type of people you are looking to meet, such as executives in higher education publishing, growth-minded CEOs in the technology industry, and the like. When people offer to give you names, ask them if they would be willing to make a "warm" introduction for you, either by speaking with the person or doing an email introduction for you. I've included some email templates at the end of the book that you can use for yourself or give to your contacts if they need help finding the best way to make the introduction.

A former publishing colleague contacted me recently to ask my advice about starting a business in human resources (HR) coaching and consulting. She asked many good questions about my business and also mentioned that she might start the business on the side while continuing to work in HR for a company. In the course of the conversation, I learned that she was losing her job with her current company, and toward the end of our talk she said, "If you run into anybody looking to hire a vice president of HR, let me know." Because that is such a broad statement, I had a difficult time thinking of anyone to whom I might introduce her. I told her it was important to develop specificity around her search. Eventually, through conversations in which I asked her about her ideal job, we narrowed her search to growth-oriented biopharmaceutical companies run by CEOs who believed in investing in the human capital of the business. With that level of specificity, I was able to give her a lead to a "link"—someone who specialized in PR for biotech companies, who potentially would have contacts for her in companies within her area of interest.

WORKSHEETS for THIS CHAPTER

See the Appendix at the back of this book for the following additional material(s) to help you work through this chapter's contents:
- Worksheet 4: Your "Natural Network"—Your Contacts
- Worksheet 5: Tips for Successful Networking Conversations
- Worksheet 6: Tracking Your Referrals
- Worksheet 7: How to Follow Up on a Warm or Semi-Warm Referral
- Worksheet 8: Email Follow-Up To Confirm A Scheduled Meeting
- Worksheet 9: Sample Phone Call or Email Asking Someone to Meet With You

CHAPTER 7

Learning to Ask Great Questions: Making the Most of Your Meetings with Networking Contacts

Now that you've created a weekly plan for connecting with people, how do you approach the conversation? This chapter offers practical pointers to help you focus your efforts and make the most of your networking conversations.

Questions: The Key to Conversation

Sales trainer Patricia Fripp says, "The key to connection is conversation. The key to conversation is questions. Therefore, learn to ask great questions." I once witnessed a great example of connecting through questions at a focus group.

The moderator was speaking with a participant before the focus group started, and within five minutes of meeting each other, the two discovered through natural questioning that one had a daughter and the other had a nephew who both attended the same college in South Carolina. Better still, the moderator had just met the nephew on the daughter's campus the previous weekend, because both were from Baltimore and had connected thanks to their Baltimore roots. What an amazing connection!

Relationships build quickly when people feel connected. Your job search is a direct result of connected relationships. Deepening your connections is a key part of landing your dream job, and connections will deepen naturally when you are genuinely interested in other people.

The Three Ps

One strategy that helps bring structure and focus to your conversations involves giving the person you're talking with a brief verbal overview of what you want to discuss at the start of the conversation. This overview creates clear expectations for your time spent conversing and also communicates to the other person that you value his or her time. A framework that I find works equally well for both telephone and in-person meetings is the three Ps: purpose, process, and payoff. Let's look at each in turn.

> PURPOSE: This is the reason you want to have the conversation. For example, you might say, "I'd like to talk with you about my career transition and job search. You're someone I respect, so I'd like to get your advice about how I should go about the search. I'd also appreciate knowing if there's anyone else you think I should speak with after I speak with you."
>
> PROCESS: The process focuses on the structure of the conversation. For example: "I'd like to give you a quick overview of where I am in my transition, learn more about how you landed your current job, and get your thoughts about what you believe I should do to find a fulfilling role in an organization."
>
> PAYOFF: The payoff reflects your goal for the conversation or the result you want to achieve from the discussion. For example: "Because I'm looking to expand my network, at the end of the conversation I'm going to ask you for one, two, or three

names of other people who might be good resources for me as I go through this process."

Here's an example of the entire three-part process for an initial contact with someone:

> "Hi, Joe; thanks for agreeing to speak with me. I'm in the middle of a job transition and would like your advice [*purpose*]. I'd like to learn a little bit about you and your work and share a bit about what type of work I'm seeking [*process*]. I'd also like to get your advice about how you might approach the job search if you were in my shoes and find out whether there are any other people you recommend I speak with after this conversation [*payoff*]. How does that sound?"

It's important to know that there is no right or wrong way to approach a conversation—there are only effective and ineffective conversations. Each time you have one of these conversations, take 10 to 15 minutes at the end of the conversation to evaluate what went well and what, if anything, you will do differently to be more effective in your next conversation. Practicing and learning from your mistakes will help you keep improving all of your future interactions.

A Fourth "P"

After you let the person know your "PPP," the next step involves one more "p": putting the focus on your conversation partner. Asking open-ended questions is the most effective way to do this, because it gets the other person talking and gives you the opportunity to learn more about him or her. We'll return to open-ended questions in the next section. For now, an aside is in order about why it's so important to focus on the other person.

When I was in elementary school, I observed on numerous occasions that everyone was drawn to my mom. My mother was the secretary to the chief of police in the town where I grew up. It fascinated me that people were so drawn to her. What I finally realized is that my mother always approached the conversation as if that person, at that moment, was the most important person in the world. She gave people the greatest gift you can give someone—the gift of active listening.

I learned a valuable lesson by observing my mom, and overall, I now recommend spending 80 to 90 percent of your conversation time listening to the other person and only 10 to 20 percent of the time speaking about your own needs. Most of us talk too much and are busy thinking about what we want to say or what we hope to gain from the conversation, rather than focusing on the other person. You will **ALWAYS** make stronger connections when you spend most of your time learning about the other person.

You're probably thinking, "Doesn't the other person need to know all about me if they're going to help me?" The answer is no! As Maya Angelou famously said, "I've learned that people will forget what you said, people will forget what you did, but people will never forget how you made them feel." It may seem counterintuitive, but other people will find you much more interesting and will be more likely to help you if you are genuinely interested in them and give them the opportunity to share their knowledge and advice. Think about how you feel when you meet someone and they are truly interested in you, your family, what you do for work, and other facets of your life. You are likely to feel appreciated and excited to be speaking with that person.

In building my own business, during a one- or two-hour conversation I typically ask questions and listen for at least 90 percent of the time. Often, people are so grateful that I'm interested in them that they ask me, without my ever bringing it up, how they can work with me. Many people don't have anyone who is truly interested in them, and your attentive listening will cause you to stand out and be different.

How to Get the Other Person Talking

So what's the best way to get your conversation partner talking? In my experience, it's asking great open-ended questions.

An open-ended question is one that requires a more in-depth response from the other person than a simple yes-or-no answer. Yes/no questions tend to generate quick, short responses that hit a dead end. Open-ended questions often start with the following words:

Who...?
What ...?
Where...?
When...?
How...?
Why...?*

I've marked "why" with an asterisk because I recommend you use this word with caution. Starting a question with *why* can put people on the defensive, leading them to respond to your question in a closed, guarded manner. There are times when it's appropriate to begin a question with *why,* but I advise you to do so sparingly.

Some people consider asking questions to be a form of prying into other people's lives, and they feel uncomfortable asking "personal" questions. If you are uncomfortable asking questions of a personal nature, there are many neutral questions you can ask that will still help you gather information:

- How did you get started in your business?
- What do you like most about your business?

- When did you realize you were interested in [your job area]?
- Where do you see your business going in the future?

Peeling the Onion

The open-ended questions you begin with are simply "launch" questions—questions that will get you started off in the conversation. After you ask a launch question, the next step is to start what I call "peeling the onion." You do this by asking questions that springboard off the responses the person just gave you.

In a literal sense, when you peel an onion, you keep removing layers until you reach as deep into the onion as you choose. In conversation, you stay focused on each "layer" until you feel it's complete and then continue to "peel" to gain more information. The more information you learn from someone, the better equipped you will be to see how he or she might be able to help you, and to find out the names of other people this person knows who might be helpful to you. For instance, if someone tells me that he or she likes an organization's work environment, I might ask, "What part of the work environment do you like?" or, "How does your current work environment differ from the ones where you've worked in the past?"

Notice that these are all open-ended questions that will generate much more information than would a similar question phrased to evoke a yes/no response—for instance, if you had asked instead, "Have you always liked your work environment?" A question phrased thus would likely evoke a simple yes or no, and you would have missed out on insights about the person to whom you are speaking. When asking questions, wording is everything!

ACTION STEP: ENGAGING THROUGH QUESTIONS
Week One: Spend 15 minutes every day engaging with someone in your family or workplace by asking open-ended questions.
Week Two: Increase your time spent asking open-ended questions to 30 minutes a day.

Continue practicing until you feel comfortable and you are naturally asking "launch" and "peel the onion" questions.

The box at the end of this chapter contains a list of Worksheets designed to help you engage your conversation partner in meaningful conversation. You'll find the worksheets in the Appendix at the end of this book.

The Power of Active Listening

After you've asked your conversation partner a question, the next step—a critically important one—is for you to listen actively and attentively. When you listen actively, you tune in not only to the words the other person is saying but also to the feelings and attitudes he or she is expressing, both verbally and nonverbally.

If you're focused on what you're going to say next, rather than on listening to the other person and determining what else you'd find interesting to learn from him or her, your conversation will be much less effective. Have you ever been around someone who starts asking you another question before you can get your response to the first question out of your mouth, or who starts talking before you've finished answering? How do you feel when your conversation partner is distracted, focused on him- or herself, or not genuinely listening? Few things in a conversation are more frustrating, and few things will shut one down faster. I can't state this too strongly:

The greatest gift you can give another person is to listen carefully and attentively.

Asking open-ended questions, listening actively and attentively to the answers, and asking additional questions based on what you've already heard will demonstrate to the other person that you genuinely care about what he or she has to say. Everyone has something of value to say—consider it your job to find out the most interesting thing about that person.

Becoming a more effective listener is a skill that can be learned through practice. It's also a great life skill in general, whether or not you're in a career transition.

WORKSHEETS for THIS CHAPTER

See the Appendix at the back of this book for the following additional material(s) to help you work through this chapter's contents:
- Worksheet 10: Asking Open-Ended Questions
- Worksheet 11: One-to-One Connector Cheat Sheet
- Worksheet 12: Fail-proof Connecting Questions
- Worksheet 13: Interview Questions

CHAPTER 8

Creating Your Plan and Sticking to It: The Right Level of Activity for You

Now that you understand why it's important to get clear about what you want to do with your career, why it matters that you believe it's possible to land a job you love, and how to tap into your network, it's time to put it all together and create a plan that you will follow consistently and persistently. First, though, I want to stress this:

Small actions, taken consistently every day, will lead you to positive outcomes, create momentum, and build your confidence.

Keep At It

When starting something new, most of us wish we could know the outcome before we begin the process—we'd like to be sure things are going to work out the way we want. Although this is unrealistic and none of us can control the outcome, we *can* control our actions and thereby influence the outcome.

No matter what the endeavor, becoming successful at it takes time and practice. When you learned to drive a car, for example, you didn't get into the car the first time and start driving as if you'd been driving for years. You probably struggled to figure out where to put your feet, how to check the rear view and side view mirrors, how to stay between the white lines on the road, how to keep the right amount of distance between you and the car in front of you, and so on.

So it is with landing your dream job: the same degree of practice and engagement is necessary. You can't wish it into existence—getting there is a process, and you MUST take the necessary actions EVERY day!

Keep It Positive

>*I don't have time for that kind of commitment—I'm already working full time.*
>
>*I don't know where to start.*
>
>*I don't want to impose on other people.*
>
>*I'm confused about what I really want to be doing.*

Do any of these thoughts sound familiar? If so, you are not alone. It's normal to have such thoughts—the important thing is to realize that they are limiting and counterproductive and not buy into them! In order to reach your goal of finding a job you love, you must become willing to recognize and change your thought process.

Focus instead on what you CAN do. Are you able to speak with only one or two people a month? Then go ahead and do that—it's still better than no action at all. The more frequently you engage with others, though, the more likely you will be to land your dream job quickly. Remember, looking for a job is a contact sport!

Keep It Real

Your best chance of success comes when you set specific goals for the individual steps you will take—steps that are realistic for you and to which you are willing to commit.

It's essential for you to feel that you are moving successfully toward finding a new job. If you set an unrealistic goal and then don't meet it, you're likely to feel that you're failing, and then you'll stop doing anything. This is why "keeping it real" is so important.

In your plan, you will specify these components:

- The amount of time you will dedicate to creating clarity about what is your ideal ("dream") job.
- A list of the contacts in your network who might be able to help you with your job search.
- The number of people you are willing to contact each week.
- The number of people with whom you are willing to meet each week.

The Appendix at the end of this book contains a worksheet to help you formulate your plan for finding your dream job.

Break It Down

I'm a big believer in breaking things down into small steps, and I'm especially fond of the number three, because breaking a bigger task down into three smaller actions or steps makes the task seem much more manageable. For instance, if I were still employed full-time at the beginning of my job search, I might focus on the following three tasks for a week or two at the outset:

1. Identify my strengths.
2. Create my energize/de-energize list.
3. Make a list of all the contacts I know.

After completing these first three actions, I might then go on to commit to two additional goals:

1. Contact five to six people every week.

2. Have breakfast, lunch, or a phone call with one to two people every week.

If I were out of work and needed to find a job quickly, I would likely double these numbers to help me achieve my goal in less time.

Remember, this process is going to take time. Depending on the level of job you are seeking, you can expect to spend 3 to 12 months landing your dream job. This time frame is broad because there are many variables: the type of job you are seeking, salary level, your level of job-seeking activity, your degree of job specialization, and other factors. As an example, in the late 1990s I landed an executive level job in 6 months, but I made my job search a full-time pursuit. When I started building my business (a version of looking for a job), I landed my first paying clients in 3 months.

WORKSHEETS for THIS CHAPTER

See the Appendix at the back of this book for the following additional material(s) to help you work through this chapter's contents:
- Worksheet 14: Dream Job Plan

CHAPTER 9

Wrapping It Up: Reviewing Lessons Learned and Putting Your Plan into Action

Now that you've come to the end of this book, where do you go from here?

My hope is that you will have completed the exercises as you read each chapter. If you have not yet done the exercises, then I recommend that you work through the book a second time and complete them as you do so. I can give you all the advice in the world, but remember: If you don't do the work, this book becomes just another "shelf help" book.

To Recap

Here are the highlights of what we've covered:

❧ **MY BEST ADVICE**
- Start by being true to yourself.
- Determine what type of job will provide the greatest alignment for you—a job that will be a natural expression of your strengths and talents, one that lets you put them to their highest and best use.

- Find a job that gives you energy on a daily basis. Remember that even though not all aspects of a job may energize you, you will feel much more fulfilled if you land a job in which you feel energized at least 80% of the time.
- Get crystal clear about the type of work you are seeking, and be specific about it! The more specific you are, the easier it will be for people to help you. Clarity is a decision—it isn't something that just happens. You create it for yourself.

MANAGE YOUR MINDSET

I hope that by now you're convinced that mindset is the key to everything that happens in your life. It's particularly important to manage your mindset and belief system on a daily basis while searching for your dream job. You can't control the outcome, but you can control what you think about, what actions you take, and how consistently you take them.

CHOOSE YOUR BELIEFS

Evaluate any belief systems that might be sabotaging your efforts. We ALL have self-limiting beliefs and stories we've either made up about ourselves or taken on from others in our lives, and those stories generally are not true. You have a choice: either let your limiting beliefs rule you, or intentionally create beliefs that will empower you. Either one will become your reality. Which reality do you choose?

BUILD YOUR CONNECTIONS

Building your connections and your social network will dramatically increase the likelihood and speed of finding your dream job. You need to continually expand your network and your contact list, because looking for a job is a contact sport. The more people you interact with, and the more frequently you interact with them, the more likely you'll be to land your dream job quickly. Action will set you free!

ASK GREAT QUESTIONS

While you're out connecting, networking, and even conversing in your everyday life, practice asking great questions. The easiest way to influence someone is to ask questions, listen, and demonstrate a genuine interest in them. People will feel much more connected to you when you make an authentic effort to learn about them, give them the stage, listen attentively to what they say, and ask for their advice.

FOLLOW YOUR PLAN

You now have a process, the tools, and a plan to find and land your dream job. Keep the plan you've created front and center, and follow it with determination. Just as elite athletes do, review your plan EVERY DAY! You might need to course correct along the way, and if you do, update the plan with your changes.

PAY IT FORWARD

Most importantly, once you land your dream job, be sure to pay it forward. Help others who are in career transition by connecting them with your contacts or by giving them a copy of this book.

* * * * *

I am committed to the belief that everyone should have fulfilling work, because fulfilling work leads to fulfilled lives.

My wish for you is that you will find and land your dream job. When you do, please email me at susan@susankatzadvantage.com to let me know about your new job and how the book helped you find and land it.

I wish you great success!

For more about Susan Katz, her coaching services, and other resources for success, visit her website at **www.susankatzadvantage.com**.

Appendix

CHAPTER 2 - WORKSHEET 1:

Strengths

From your perspective, what type of activities and work do you do best?

_____

_____

_____

_____

From other people's perspective (friends, family, co-workers, etc.), what would they say about the type of work you do best?

_____

_____

_____

_____

Create Your Dream Job: Change Your Mindset, Change Your Future

CHAPTER 2 - WORKSHEET 2:

Energizing & De-Energizing Activities

Energizing Acitivities	De-Energizing Activities

CHAPTER 3 - WORKSHEET 3:

A Day at Your Dream Job

Imagine it's one year from now and you've landed your dream job. Write a description of "a day in your life" at your new job. Think about how it feels to wake up in the morning and get ready for work, how you feel when you travel to and arrive at work, what type of work you are doing, with whom you are interacting, and the type of feedback you are receiving for all the great work you are doing.

_____
_____
_____
_____
_____
_____
_____
_____
_____
_____
_____
_____
_____
_____
_____
_____
_____
_____
_____
_____

CHAPTER 6 - WORKSHEET 4:

Your "Natural Network" – Your Contacts

List all of the contacts in "your world" who might be able to lead you to other "links" or contacts. Think of family, friends, colleagues, neighbors, people you know from volunteer activities, etc. Do NOT screen out the people you put onto your list. Write down as many people as possible!

CONTACT NAME	CONTACT INFORMATION

CONTACT NAME	CONTACT INFORMATION

CHAPTER 6 - WORKSHEET 5:

Tips for Successful Networking Conversations

Overview

There are two primary types of networking: networking events and one-to-one networking meetings. All networking is designed to help you build and enhance relationships that may eventually lead to doing business with someone or identifying connections in another person's network.

When you attend a networking event, your goal is to meet one, two, or three people with whom you can schedule a follow-up meeting. It's not the time to "sell" or spend all your time handing out business cards.

Starting conversations at either a networking event or in a one-to-one meeting may feel awkward and uncomfortable. If that's how you feel, then you are in good company, as most people experience a degree of discomfort, especially at networking events. Sometimes people feel this way because they are afraid they might ask the wrong questions, they might sound pushy or intrusive, or they might get answers they don't want to hear.

The key to minimizing your discomfort is to stay focused on the person to whom you are speaking. Set an intention to find out what's most interesting about them. By doing that, you will take the pressure off yourself while building a relationship. The best advice I ever received and that I still find useful in networking situations is to show up being "interested," not "interesting."

Here are some tactics for being "interested":
- Follow the "80/20" rule. Listen at least 80% of the time and talk no more than 20% of the time. The more you talk, the less engaged and connected the other person will be. The more you listen, the more engaged and connected the other person will be — and the more they will want to continue building a relationship with you.
- Follow the "WAIT" principle. Ask yourself, "**W**hy **A**m **I T**alking?" It's a reminder to stay focused on what the other person has to say. The WAIT principle applies to many forms of communication, not just networking events or networking meetings.
- Ask open-ended questions. A great way to learn about another person is to ask open-ended questions. Remember to be genuine and listen carefully to the responses. Your questions will naturally evolve from what the person tells you. Good open-ended questions that get people talking usually begin with words like "what," "when," "who," "where," "why," and "how."

Sample Questions
1. What brought you to the event?
2. What business are you in?
3. What's your role in the organization?
4. How did you get into your business?
5. Where did you work previously?
6. What type of people do you hope to meet at the event?
7. If I could introduce you to one person at the event, who would that be?
8. What other events do you attend?

Use these questions to "peel the onion" and learn more about the other person. Continue peeling the onion by asking more questions based upon what the person just told you, so be sure you actively listen to the person's responses.

If you ever feel stuck in a conversation and don't know what to ask next, simply say:
- Tell me more about (whatever they were just telling you about)…
- Help me understand (whatever they were just telling you about)…

As practiced as I am at asking questions and listening, these statements often help me when I'm at a loss for the next question.

Moving the conversation to a one-to-one meeting

Decide in advance what you would like to accomplish at a networking event. Think about the following:
- With whom (what type of people) would you like to build relationships?
- For my purposes, I am interested in meeting potential referral sources, prospective clients, and anyone who I believe is well connected and would be a good person to know, or someone who just seems interesting.
- What are the characteristics of your target client? For example, because I work with small business owners who've been in business for at least three years and have a minimum of two employees, I am looking to identify those people during my brief 5-10 minute conversation with them.

I'm a big believer in "permission-based" questions because they feel less pushy and offer the other person a choice of saying yes or no when you ask them to do something for you (like schedule a meeting with you). There is a fine distinction, though, between using the word "would" vs. "could" —"would" is the stronger and more effective of the two words. Once you have identified someone as a good contact and someone you would like to speak with again, here's what you would say:

"I've really enjoyed speaking with you. I believe there might be some good opportunities for us to help each other and I'd like to learn more about you and your business. Would you be open to scheduling a coffee, breakfast, or lunch meeting?"

Decide which meeting type (coffee, breakfast, or lunch) you are going to suggest based upon the meeting priority level. Use coffee meetings for lower priority meetings, and breakfast or lunch for higher priorities because they offer you more time with the person. If the person says yes, say:

"Rather than playing phone or email tag, would it make sense to check our calendars now to schedule a time to meet?"

Another sure-fire way to get someone to meet with you is to offer to introduce them to other people in your network who might be prospective clients or referral sources for them. Here's what you would say in that situation:

"I would like to learn more about you and your business so I can introduce you to people in my network who might benefit from knowing you or from your services. Would you be interested in meeting for coffee, breakfast or lunch?"

Once you schedule a meeting, use the same questions and philosophy that you used at the networking event-the 80/20 rule and the WAIT principle, for example. If you continue to ask questions, learn about others, and find ways to help add value, you will build strong relationships with people who will remember you when they have someone to refer for your services.

CHAPTER 6 - WORKSHEET 6:

Tracking Your Referrals

This list will help you keep track of the referrals you receive from each person to whom you speak or with whom you meet.

CONTACT (Referral Souce)	CONTACT INFO AND DATE CONTACTED

CHAPTER 6 - WORKSHEET 7:

How to Follow Up on A Warm or Semi-Warm Referral

When you are meeting with your "connections," or the people who are going to help you connect to others-and who in turn will help you connect and make forward progress in your job search -people will offer to refer you to people they know and suggest that you connect.

When this happens, they are likely to give you a name and contact info. You should do the following

1. Ask the person with whom you are meeting if he would be willing to make a warm introduction by phone or email.
2. If someone agrees to connect you by phone or email, ask, "By when do you anticipate having time to make the introduction and connection?" Then, if the date comes and goes, you can follow up and remind him that he was going to make a connection for you. Gently remind him by saying something like, "Thanks for offering to make an introduction for me to *(name of person)*. I really appreciate your willingness to connect them to me. Have you had an opportunity tospeak with or email *(name of person)* about me? If not, I look forward to hearing from you as soon as you are able to do so."
3. If they prefer to just give you a name and contact information and tell you to contact them using their

name, you will contact the person directly (by phone and/or email) and say the following:

"(*Name of person*) suggested I contact you. (*Name of person*) thought you would be a good contact for me as part of my job search. I am not contacting you for a job but I would like to get your advice about my search. Would you be willing to take 15-20 minutes to speak with me and share some of your advice? I am seeking information about how you would approach the search, if you were in my shoes, and perhaps if you know of any other people to whom I should speak. I appreciate your consideration and I look forward to hearing from you."

(Include this last sentence if you are writing this rather than contacting the person by phone.)

CHAPTER 6 - WORKSHEET 8:

Email Follow-Up To Confirm a Scheduled Meeting

After you have spoken on the phone with someone who agreed to give you 15- 20 minutes of their time to help with your job search, you should follow up with an email to say thanks and set up the next meeting. Here is a sample:

Dear *(Name of person)*,

Thanks for agreeing to meet with me on *(day and date)*. I appreciate your willingness to help me in my job search by offering your advice.

I've attached a copy of my resume by way of some background. During our conversation, I would like to:
1. Learn how you got started in your (career/profession)
2. Learn what you like about your work
3. Tell you a bit about what type of work I am seeking
4. Get your advice about how you would go about the search if you were in my situation.

I am interested in hearing your suggestions for how I should approach my job search more effectively.

Thanks in advance and I look forward to seeing you on *(date and time)*

Sincerely,
Name
Contact Info

CHAPTER 6 - WORKSHEET 9:

Sample Phone Call or Email Asking Someone to Meet With You

The best way to secure an appointment with someone is to call. If you are unable to reach someone by phone, leave a voice message and send a follow up email. You can use this script for the phone call, the email, or both.

Hi (*name of person*),

(If you called and left a message, say: "I recently left you a voice message.")

I am currently in the process of a job search and thought you would be a good person to give me advice about my search. I am not contacting you for a job. I value your opinion and would like your thoughts and insights about different careers and the best way to approach my job search. I would appreciate 15-20 minutes of your time.

Would you be available to meet on one of the following dates and times?

Date and time
Date and time
Date and time

Thanks in advance for your consideration. I look forward to hearing from you soon.

Sincerely
Name
Contact information

CHAPTER 7 – WORKSHEET 10:

Dream Job Plan

Open-ended questions begin with the following words:
- WHAT
- WHERE
- WHO
- WHEN
- HOW
- WHY

Five open-ended questions I will routinely ask are:

1. _____

_____

_____

_____

_____

2. _____

_____

_____

_____

_____

3. _____

_____

_____

_____

4. _____
_____
_____
_____
_____

5. _____
_____
_____
_____
_____

Three people with whom I will practice are:

1. _____
_____
_____
_____
_____

2. _____
_____
_____
_____
_____

3. _____
_____
_____
_____
_____

CHAPTER 7 - WORKSHEET 11:

One-to-One Connector Cheat Sheet

When you finally secure a meeting with someone for 15 to 20 minutes, you need to give them an overview of what you would like to accomplish in the conversation.

For example, say:

"Thank you for taking time to meet with me. I would like to spend some time learning about you and how you got involved in your business, give you a brief overview of what type of work I'm looking for, get your advice on what you would do if you were in my shoes, and identify one or two other people who you believe would be good resources for me in my job search."

After you have laid out your agenda, ask some key questions -and remember to listen to what the other person has to say, asking questions based upon what they tell you.

You might start with:
- How did you get started in your profession/career?
- What do you like best about your work?
- If you had it to do over again, what would you do differently?

Here's what asking questions based upon close listening might look like:

If the other person tells you she became interested in a career as an accountant because she took a college accounting course that piqued her interest, you mighT ask, "What, if any, other options did you consider?"

There are other types of follow-up questions to ask, as well. The key is to listen intently, be focused on the other person, and be genuinely interested in learning about them and how they got to their current position.

The most effective way to engage with and have other people help you is to remain interested in them. By doing that, you will begin building strong and lasting relationships. People will remember you more from the quality of your questions and how you listen rather than what you specifically have to tell them about yourself.

CHAPTER 7 - WORKSHEET 12:

Fail-Proof Connecting Questions

When you prepare for a phone or in-person job interview, you should review the requirements of the job and prepare in advance by answering the following questions:

Job Requirements:
- What is the job description that is noted in the position description?
- What skills are required for the position?

Your Skills:
- What skills do you have that match the job requirements?
- Where do you notice that you are missing skills?
- How will you acquire or address the areas where you are missing skills?

Demonstrate Skills:

What stories can you tell from past jobs that demonstrate your skills?

Use the chart on the next page to complete your analysis.

Create Your Dream Job: Change Your Mindset, Change Your Future

Job Requirements	Your Skills	Examples From Past Jobs

Chapter 7 - Worksheet 13:

Interview Questions

During your job search process, you will have telephone and in-person interviews. It is important to use the interview time to answer questions AND to ask questions of the interviewer, to be sure the job is a fit for you. In other words, you will both be interviewing each other.

If the interview is a preliminary screening interview by phone, focus on answering the interviewer's questions, rather than asking too many questions, because the interview is likely to be very brief. It's best to save your questions for an in-person interview.

One of the best ways to prepare for an interview is to role-play with a family member or friend. Have them ask you the questions that an interviewer might ask, and take the time to think through, write down, and practice answering the interview questions. Keep your answers succinct and avoid going off on a tangent about any particular topic. After you answer the questions in your practice session, have the person give feedback about your answers by telling you what worked well and what changes they would recommend to make you more effective.

Sample interviewer questions:
1. Why are you interested in this job?
2. Why do you believe you are qualified for the position?
3. What are your greatest strengths?
4. What's your biggest weakness?

5. Tell me about a project that you were most proud of and why.
6. Tell me about a time when there was a problem with a coworker and how you handled it.

Another way to prepare for this process is to pretend you already landed the job. Ask yourself, "What would I want to know to be as successful as possible if I were in the position?"

Sample interviewee questions:
1. How did this position open up? (or, if the position is new) How was this position created?
2. What does a typical day look like for this position?
3. What have others in the position done well?
4. How does this position fit with the growth plans of the company?
5. How will you measure success in this position?
6. What are the three most important characteristics or skills that the person needs for the job?
7. Based upon our conversation, how well do you believe I would fit with the position?
8. When do you plan to make a hiring decision?

It is important throughout the interview to ask "peel-the-onion" questions.

Instead of just answering the interviewer's question, focus on asking questions that will help both you and the interviewer determine if you are a fit for the job. This is an opportunity for both you and the interviewer to gain greater clarity. Never assume you know what the other person means about a particular topic.

For example, if the interviewer says to you that teamwork is important, a peel-the-onion question might be, "What do you mean by teamwork?" or "What does teamwork look like in your organization?" If the interviewer mentions that collaboration is important, you might ask, "What does collaboration look like in your organization?" or "What's a good example of the type of collaboration that has occurred in the organization?"

If after learning about the position you are still interested, be sure to communicate that to the interviewer. For example, you might say, "I am very interested in this position. When should I expect to hear about your hiring decision? What would be the best way for me to follow up with you?"

Interviewing for a job can be stressful, but if you prepare and practice in advance you will be much more likely to enjoy the process. When you enjoy the process, you are likely to be perceived much more favorably, which will increase your opportunities for being hired in a job that's a great fit for both you and the employer.

CHAPTER 8 - WORKSHEET 14:

Dream Job Plan

1. My clearly articulated statement (what I am going to tell people about the work I would like to do) is :

_____
_____
_____
_____
_____
_____
_____
_____

2. The top 10 key connections I need to contact in the next 30 days are:

_____
_____
_____
_____
_____
_____
_____
_____
_____
_____

3. The number of calls I will make to schedule appointments each week is:

_____
_____
_____
_____
_____

4. The way I will ask others for referrals to people who can help me in my job search is:

_____
_____
_____
_____
_____
_____
_____
_____

Create Your Dream Job: Change Your Mindset, Change Your Future

www.ingramcontent.com/pod-product-compliance
Lightning Source LLC
Chambersburg PA
CBHW070630300426
44113CB00010B/1721